Contents

Introduction

"Imhotep is half-dead and he will be half-dead for all time. Nobody can bring him and Anck-su-namun back to the world of the living, or he will make everybody in the world his mummies. And the scarabs will fly again and eat us all. It will be the end of the world."

Imhotep and his lover Anck-su-namun lived in Egypt at the time of the Pharaoh Seti the First. After that, for more than three thousand years, they were dead—but not dead.

Then, some people find them. O'Connell is a wild American soldier. Evelyn is a quiet, intelligent British woman; her world is books, not guns and fighting. In the Egyptian desert, O'Connell and Evelyn find Imhotep, and they also find love. But they don't know Imhotep's story.

Will Imhotep and Anck-su-namun live again? And will that be the end of the world for all of us? Or will O'Connell, Evelyn, and their friends send them back to the dead?

The Mummy is a book and also a movie (Universal, 1999) by Stephen Sommers. In the movie, Brendan Fraser is O'Connell, Rachel Weisz is Evelyn, Arnold Vosloo is Imhotep, and John Hannah is Evelyn's brother, Jonathan. Universal Films made the first movie of *The Mummy* in 1932.

The Mummy

Adapted by
DAVID LEVITHAN
Based on the screenplay by
STEPHEN SOMMERS

Level 2

Retold by Mike Dean
Series Editors: Andy Hopkins and Jocelyn Potter

Pearson Education Limited
Edinburgh Gate, Harlow,
Essex CM20 2JE, England
and Associated Companies throughout the world.

ISBN: 978-1-4058-8169-2

First published by Scholastic Ltd, 1999
Penguin Books edition first published 2001
This edition first published 2008

3 5 7 9 10 8 6 4 2

Typeset by Graphicraft Ltd, Hong Kong
Set in 11/14pt Bembo
Printed in China
SWTC/02

Pen

For a complete list of the titles available in the Penguin Readers series please write to your local
Pearson Longman office or to: Penguin Readers Marketing Department, Pearson Education,
Edinburgh Gate, Harlow, Essex CM20 2JE, England.

Chapter 1   Anck-su-namun

Thebes, Egypt, 1290 BC[*]

Thebes was the city of Imhotep, the High Priest of the Dead. It was also the city of Anck-su-namun. Anck-su-namun was the Pharaoh's[†] lover. But she loved Imhotep.

Imhotep walked into her bedroom and took the beautiful woman in his arms.

"My love for you is more important than life," he said.

Outside the bedroom door, Imhotep's priests watched. But when Pharaoh Seti the First of Egypt walked in, they couldn't stop him.

Imhotep quickly ran into the next room. Pharaoh Seti heard something, but he didn't see him.

"Who was here?" Seti asked Anck-su-namun. "I know somebody was here, in your bedroom."

And then, the Pharaoh looked into the next room.

"Imhotep!" he said. "My High Priest!"

Anck-su-namun looked at Imhotep. They had to kill the Pharaoh before the Pharaoh and his soldiers killed them. Anck-su-namun took her knife and pushed it hard into the Pharaoh's back. The Pharaoh's eyes opened wide. Then, Imhotep took the Pharaoh's sword and killed him.

They heard something outside. The Pharaoh's soldiers—the Med-Jai—were there. But Imhotep's priests came in first. They took the Pharaoh's sword from Imhotep's hand.

[*]BC: before Christ was born
[†]Pharaoh: the name for an Egyptian king in old times

1

"Come with us," the priests said to him. "Quick." They pulled him away from his lover.

"No!" said Imhotep. "I will stay with Anck-su-namun."

"Please go," said Anck-su-namun. "Please live. They will kill me, but you can bring me back to life. Only you, the High Priest, can do it."

The priests took Imhotep with them. The Pharaoh's soldiers ran in. Anck-su-namun didn't say goodbye to Imhotep; there wasn't time. She took the Pharaoh's sword and pushed it into her heart.

Imhotep saw her die.

◆

The Pharaoh's soldiers found Anck-su-namun's knife in the Pharaoh's back. But they didn't find Imhotep in her room. So Imhotep, the High Priest, had to send his lover—the killer of the Pharaoh—to the underworld.

Imhotep had to mummify Anck-su-namun. First, he cut out her heart. He put it in a gold box. Then, he read from the gold *Book of Amun Ra*. The *Book of Amun Ra* sent the bad people of this world to the underworld, a dark place with no hope.

They all watched her go—the Med-Jai, the people of Egypt, and the priests. Only the priests, with their white cats, weren't afraid. Nobody could hurt the priests when their white cats were with them.

But Imhotep could bring his lover back—back from the underworld, back from the dead.

◆

The *Book of the Dead* could bring Anck-su-namun back. This black book was in the statue of the god Anubis. It was Anubis's book—a book for gods, not for men. But for his lover—for Anck-su-namun—Imhotep didn't listen to gods.

2

Imhotep, the High Priest of the Dead.

The statue of Anubis was at Hamunaptra, the City of the Dead. Egypt's gold was there, too. Late at night Imhotep took his dead lover, Anck-su-namun, there. He also took her heart, in its gold box. He went across the desert to Hamunaptra on horseback with his priests.

There were ten soldiers at the statue of Anubis. But Imhotep was the High Priest, so the soldiers helped him. They carried dead Anck-su-namun. Imhotep and his priests found the *Book of the Dead*, and they took it to an underground room—a room of the dead. The soldiers followed.

When Imhotep began to read from the *Book of the Dead*, Anck-su-namun's heart moved, in its gold box. There was life in it again. Then, Anck-su-namun opened her eyes.

"Nothing can stop me now," thought Imhotep.

But he was wrong.

The Med-Jai from Thebes ran into the underground room with swords in their hands. They stopped Imhotep. They broke the box with Anck-su-namun's heart in it, and Anck-su-namun died again.

◆

The Med-Jai mummified Imhotep's twenty-one priests, and Imhotep had to watch. They made the ten soldiers from Hamunaptra into mummies, too. They put them all into the ground before they were dead.

But for Imhotep there was something worse than that. First, they cut out his eyes with knives. Then, they put him into the ground—a mummy before he was dead. But that wasn't the worst thing. They put scarabs on Imhotep's face. The scarabs ran into his mouth and nose and started to eat him. This was Hom Dai, or half-life.

"The scarabs will eat him for all time," said the Med-Jai. "Imhotep is half-dead and he will be half-dead for all time.

Nobody can bring him and Anck-su-namun back to the world of the living, or he will make everybody in the world his mummies. And the scarabs will fly again and eat us all. It will be the end of the world.

"So we, the Med-Jai, will stay here and watch Imhotep. First us, and then our sons, and then the sons of our sons. Nothing is more important than that."

The Med-Jai looked down at Imhotep. The scarabs started to eat him. He could never get out.

Or could he?

They carried dead Anck-su-namum.

Chapter 2   O'Connell and Evelyn

3213 years later. Hamunaptra, 1923

Most of Hamunaptra is under the desert. Only one or two houses stand in Seti the First's great City of the Dead, and in those houses some soldiers are fighting for France. They are fighting with hundreds of desert horsemen.

Again and again, the horsemen came out of the desert with the sun on their backs. They had guns and they shot at the soldiers. One of the men was a better fighter than the other soldiers. This man wasn't French. He was American and his name was Rick O'Connell.

Next to him was Beni, a Hungarian. Beni was O'Connell's friend—sometimes, when he wanted something.

"Why are you here?" O'Connell said to Beni, and he shot again.

"I took some gold from a temple," said Beni, with a smile. "And you? Why are you a soldier? Did you kill somebody?"

"No," said O'Connell. "But I'm thinking about it." And he shot another horseman from his horse.

"No, tell me," Beni said. "Why are you here in the desert?"

"I want to have a good time," said O'Connell.

The horsemen were now very close. O'Connell shot. Then, he shouted and shot again.

"There's only you and me, Beni," shouted O'Connell.

But Beni didn't answer. He wasn't there.

Four horsemen were almost on top of O'Connell. He ran. He saw Beni in front of a temple. The Hungarian went in and started to close the temple door.

"DON'T CLOSE THAT DOOR!" O'Connell shouted at Beni.

But Beni closed it in his face and O'Connell couldn't open it.

6

He was American and his name was Rick O'Connell.

Beni closed the door in his face.

atherouse

"I'm going to get you for this," O'Connell shouted at Beni, through the closed door.

But first there were four desert horsemen with guns in his face. He had a problem.

"OK," shouted O'Connell. "I'm ready. The four of you. Fight me!"

But the four horsemen didn't fight. Their horses went up on their back feet. Their ears went back and their eyes opened. They threw the four horsemen to the ground and ran away. The horsemen followed them.

"*Why?*" O'Connell thought. "*I don't understand.*"

He turned around. There, behind him, was an old statue. It was the god Anubis. Why did the horsemen run from a statue? But suddenly, he was afraid, too. A wind came across the desert. The yellow ground moved with the wind, and under it there was a big face. It was the face of the High Priest Imhotep.

8

O'Connell ran away from Hamunaptra. But there were eyes on his back in the hot desert. He knew that, he could feel them. He turned and looked up.

There, high up on a mountain, were the Med-Jai.

◆

Evelyn Carnahan was a quiet, uninteresting woman, people thought. And she worked in a quiet place. It was a place full of very old books—the Cairo Museum.

Evelyn put a book on the top shelf. She saw something up there and she was angry. She was angry because the name of the book started with the letter T. Why was it on that shelf? The other books on the shelf started with S.

Evelyn took the book from the top shelf. But she fell and the books fell with her. The bookshelf fell and hit another bookshelf. Then, that bookshelf hit the shelf behind it. In two minutes, all the old books in the museum, from A-Z, were on the floor. Evelyn fell on the floor with them.

The curator of the museum walked in.

"Oh," said Evelyn. She wasn't very happy.

"Look at this!" shouted the curator. "What are you doing? Why did we give you a job here?"

"*Oh be quiet!*" Evelyn thought. She said, "You gave me a job here because I know everything about the Pharaohs. I understand the old languages and I can read these books. I . . ."

Evelyn stopped. She felt very angry and very British, but she didn't want to lose this job. She liked living in Cairo.

The curator said some more angry words and then left.

Evelyn got up and started to put the books on the shelves again.

Somebody spoke. "I am the undead," it said.

Evelyn looked behind a shelf and saw . . . a mummy. She screamed. And then, the mummy started to laugh.

"Hello, baby sister," it said.

Her brother Jonathan put his head up. Then, he came out from behind the mummy.

"Jonathan!" He was more than thirty years old—and a baby. "Jonathan, go and put that mummy back."

"Ah, but I have something for you," said her brother.

"Oh no!"

Jonathan often found things from the time of the Pharaohs and brought them to his intelligent sister. But when people in the museum looked at them, they weren't really old.

"OK," said Evelyn. "What is it this time?"

It was a box, and the box had Egyptian writing on it. Evelyn looked at it. She opened the box carefully, and took out a key and a map.

"Jonathan," she said. "This is *very* important."

Evelyn and Jonathan took the box to the museum's curator. The curator looked at it.

"See!" said Evelyn. "It's from the time of Seti the First."

"Maybe," said the curator.

The curator wasn't excited. Evelyn couldn't understand that. Did the curator know something about the box?

"Who was Seti the First?" asked Jonathan. "Was he rich?"

"The richest of the Pharaohs," answered Evelyn.

Jonathan liked this answer. The curator looked at the map.

"This map is more than 3,000 years old," said Evelyn.

She knew a lot about the Pharaohs and she wanted the curator to forget the books on the floor.

"The writing tells us that it's a map of Hamunaptra."

The curator was afraid of the name Hamunaptra. But he turned away from Evelyn, so she didn't see his face.

"My dear girl," said the curator, "there are a lot of stories about Hamunaptra . . ."

10

"This is very important."

"Is this Hamunaptra, City of the Dead?" asked Jonathan. He and Evelyn had an Egyptian mother. They listened to stories about Hamunaptra when they were children.

"Yes," Evelyn answered. "Hamunaptra, City of the Dead. The Pharaohs put their gold there."

The curator had the map in his hands. It was above a candle on his desk. He moved his hands down.

"No!" shouted Jonathan.

He pulled the map away from the candle and put out the fire with his hand. Some of the map was black now. You couldn't see the City of the Dead.

"Why did you do that?" asked Jonathan.

"It wasn't really an old map," said the curator. "Didn't you know that, Miss Carnahan? That's very stupid of you."

11

But it *was* an old map and it showed Hamunaptra. Evelyn knew that. She took the key from the curator quickly, before he threw that away. She could ask other people about the map. But where did Jonathan get it?

Outside the curator's office, she asked her brother that question.

"Where did I get it? Oh, I took it from a man in a bar. He was an American. His name was Rick O'Connell."

◆

Evelyn and Jonathan went to the bar. Evelyn wasn't happy about that. She didn't usually go to bars and this was a very dirty bar. The American, Rick O'Connell, was there. He was always there, all day every day. He was dirty and he was ready for a fight.

"Don't I know you?" O'Connell said to Jonathan. "I saw you somewhere. And who's your little girlfriend? Very nice!"

"She's my sister," said Jonathan.

"Little . . . little . . . I am . . ." Evelyn wasn't anybody's "little girlfriend." But she didn't say that. She wanted to leave, but this man knew about the map and the key. Only O'Connell had the answers to her questions.

"We . . . er . . . found this box," she began.

"You want to know about Hamunaptra," said O'Connell.

Evelyn's eyes opened. This American wasn't stupid.

"How do you know that the box is from Hamunaptra?"

"Because I found it in Hamunaptra. I was there."

Suddenly, O'Connell remembered Jonathan. "You took my box," he said. And he hit Jonathan in the face. Jonathan fell on the floor.

"Tell me about Hamunaptra," said Evelyn.

"I hit your brother," said O'Connell. "He's on the floor. And you want to know about Hamunaptra?"

"Oh, he's OK," said Evelyn. "He's often on the floor."

O'Connell almost smiled at that. This British woman was interesting.

"I was at Hamunaptra," he said. "I was a soldier at the City of the Dead."

"What did you see?" asked Evelyn.

"I saw a lot of desert," said O'Connell. "I saw a lot of people die."

"Where is Hamunaptra?" asked Evelyn. "Can you take me there? I want to find a book. It's called the *Book of Amun Ra* and it's at Hamunaptra."

Her face was close to O'Connell's. O'Connell kissed her.

"What! Jonathan! Get up. You and I are leaving this bar."

"Thanks for the visit," shouted O'Connell, before they walked out the door.

◆

Evelyn and Jonathan went back to the museum. They walked past the curator's office, but they didn't go in. So they didn't see the man in the curator's office. The man in the office knew the curator. He knew O'Connell, too. He was high on a mountain when O'Connell ran away, into the desert. His name was Ardeth Bay and he was the head of the Med-Jai. The curator was in the Med-Jai, too.

"Miss Carnahan wants to go to Hamunaptra," said the curator.

"Stop her," said Ardeth Bay. "Stop her or kill her."

Chapter 3   The *Book of the Dead*

The sun was at her back, the wind was in her hair. Evelyn wanted to laugh and cry at the same time. She loved the desert. And the idea of Hamunaptra was exciting! She and Jonathan were near the temple now. Their horses were very tired.

Then, they saw a man outside the temple.

"Oh no!" said Evelyn.

The man said, "Can I help you down from that horse?"

"O'Connell!"

"That's me!"

"What are you doing here?"

She wanted to be angry with O'Connell, but he looked cleaner now. And maybe he could help them.

"He's here for the gold," said Jonathan.

O'Connell smiled. "Oh, I only want to have a good time," he said. And he looked into Evelyn's eyes.

More people arrived outside the temple. There were three Americans and a lot of Egyptian diggers. With them was Beni.

"You came back," O'Connell said to Beni.

Beni laughed. "You, too."

Outside the temple there were a lot of thin horses.

One of the Americans, Daniels, asked, "Where did these horses come from?"

"What are you doing here?"

14

Hamunaptra, City of the Dead.

"They're waiting," said Beni. "Sometimes people find Hamunaptra, but they all die. Their horses wait for them, but then they die, too."

◆

Beni, the Americans, and their diggers looked for a way down under the desert to the gold. Jonathan walked around the houses, but then, he found the top of the statue of Anubis. Most of the statue was under the desert.

He, Evelyn, and O'Connell started to dig down and down into the desert. They found a dark room under the ground, and they got in through a wall.

"We're the first people in this room for more than 3,000 years," said Evelyn. For her, this was wonderful.

"It's dark and cold down here," said O'Connell. He wasn't very excited.

"Where's the gold?" said Jonathan.

"*You boys don't understand*," thought Evelyn. "*We find the wonderful world of the Pharaohs and I'm with . . . them!*"

Then, they lit a candle in the room.

"Oh my God!" said Evelyn. "It's a *Sah-Netjer*."

"It's a what?" asked O'Connell.

"The priests made mummies in this room," Jonathan told him.

"The dead went to the afterlife from here," said Evelyn.

O'Connell didn't like that. He took out his gun. They walked through the dark from room to room. Some of the rooms were very small. Sometimes their candle almost went out and left them in the dark.

Then, they heard something. Evelyn looked at O'Connell.

O'Connell had his gun in front of him, and he walked slowly in the dark. He saw the bottom of the statue of Anubis, under the ground. Then, he heard something again, from the back of the statue. It came closer. And *CLOSER*.

Three people came at him. The Americans! They had guns in their hands.

"*We* want to look here," said Burns, one of the Americans.

He looked around him. He wore thick glasses.

"No, *we* want to look here," said O'Connell.

"This is *our* statue, friend," said Daniels.

"I don't see your name on it, *friend*," said O'Connell.

More guns came out now. The diggers and Beni all had guns, too.

"We have ten guns and you have one," said the Hungarian, not very nicely. "It doesn't look very good for you."

"It looked bad for me before in this city," said O'Connell. "But here I am again!"

"Er . . . Here I am, too," said Jonathan.

His face was white, but he had a small gun in his hand.

16

More guns came out now.

Beni's eyes were wild. He wanted to kill O'Connell. Evelyn put her hand over O'Connell's gun.

"Let's be nice children," she said. "And play nicely."

She pulled O'Connell away, and Jonathan followed. The Americans and Beni laughed.

"We can dig in other places," Evelyn told O'Connell.

◆

Evelyn walked down under the statue of Anubis, and Jonathan and O'Connell followed. Evelyn wanted to dig under the statue, before the Americans got into the statue from above.

They stood under the statue, and Jonathan and O'Connell started to dig into it. Above them, the Americans and their diggers started to dig into the top of the statue.

Then, they heard horses and guns.

"Stay here!" shouted O'Connell.

He got his gun and ran up to the Americans. Evelyn and Jonathan followed him. O'Connell saw Beni, the Americans, and the diggers shooting. Around them were Ardeth Bay and the Med-Jai, with their guns. O'Connell ran to Beni and started shooting at the Med-Jai.

"Oh, not again!" said Beni. "Do you *like* fighting?"

"No, but I look good when I do," said O'Connell.

And he shot a Med-Jai soldier.

Evelyn had a gun in her hand for the first time. She shot at the Med-Jai, too.

"Stop!" shouted Ardeth Bay. The Med-Jai stopped shooting. Everybody stopped shooting. It was quiet.

"LEAVE THIS PLACE!" said the head of the Med-Jai. "LEAVE THIS PLACE OR DIE!"

Ardeth Bay left, and the other Med-Jai soldiers followed him.

"There's gold here," said Daniels, when it was quiet again. "Those soldiers were here for the gold."

"No," said O'Connell. "They're desert people. Water is important to them, not gold. But there's something more important than water or gold down here."

◆

O'Connell, Jonathan, and Evelyn went back down to the bottom of the statue. The Americans and their diggers started to dig again at the top. They got into the statue and the diggers found a big box.

There was Egyptian writing on the box. Beni read it.

"Don't open this," he told the other men. The Americans laughed. "Seti the First wasn't stupid," said Beni. "The diggers can open the box. I'm out of here."

Beni knew Egypt. He understood the country's language and its gods. He was afraid and he ran.

There was Egyptian writing on the box.

"Open the box," Burns said to the diggers.

The diggers were afraid, but they opened the box. Then, they screamed. Scarabs ran out of the box. The scarabs ran into the diggers' feet, up their legs, up and up and into their brains. Then, the scarabs ate their brains. The diggers stopped screaming.

The Americans were afraid but they took the gold from the box. Beni came back into the room.

"What did that writing on the box say?" asked Henderson.

"It said,'Open this and you die.'"

◆

At the bottom of the statue, Jonathan was asleep. Evelyn and O'Connell stopped digging and sat on the floor in the dark. They were very tired. O'Connell lit a fire and looked into Evelyn's eyes. Evelyn put her face close to his.

"I'm going to kiss you, Mr. O'Connell," she said.

"No, you're not," said O'Connell.

"I'm not?"

"OK. You can. But call me 'Rick,' not 'Mr. O'Connell.'"

Evelyn smiled and put her face closer to his.

"Rick," she said and closed her eyes. "Rick."

And then, she was asleep.

O'Connell smiled. "That was nice, ma'am," he said.

◆

The next morning, they got into the top of the statue of Anubis. Inside, there was a coffin.

"Look!" Evelyn said to Jonathan. "There's no writing on this coffin, so the dead man in here isn't going to the afterlife. He's staying in this world. He did something very, very bad."

Jonathan took out the key and put it in the coffin. The coffin half-opened. O'Connell pulled the coffin open and a 3,000-year-old mummy stood up.

O'Connell, Evelyn, and Jonathan screamed. Then, the mummy fell back in its coffin. Imhotep wasn't dead, but he wasn't of this world. He was undead.

He wanted life . . .

◆

Above them, the Americans looked in the box. They wanted gold, but they found only a book. Henderson took it out.

"It's an old black book," he said.

"Be careful with that," said Beni. "It's the *Book of the Dead*."

"I don't want a book!" shouted Daniels.

He was angry and he kicked the box. The box broke and a smaller gold box fell out.

"That's better!" said Daniels.

And he took the box with Anck-su-namun's heart in it.

◆

That evening, Evelyn, Jonathan, and O'Connell walked up to the top of the statue again. They sat around a fire with the Americans. Beni was asleep . . . with the *Book of the Dead* next to him.

Evelyn tried not to take it, but it was impossible. She had to look at it. She took it and opened it. The second person in 3,000 years with the *Book of the Dead* in her hands . . . It was exciting!

"Do you think that's a good idea?" asked O'Connell.

"Oh," said Evelyn. "People read books all the time!" She looked at O'Connell. Her face said, "*I work in a museum. I know about books. And you don't!*"

Evelyn began to read to O'Connell from the book:

"*Ahm kum Ra . . .*

Ahm hum Dei . . ."

Below them, Imhotep moved. The words from the *Book of the Dead* started him on his way back to life. The scarabs started to fly again.

Evelyn began to read from the Book of the Dead.

Chapter 4   Imhotep

They could hear the scarabs, hundreds of them. And then, they saw them. They all wanted to scream, but there wasn't time. Evelyn, Jonathan, and O'Connell ran up some stairs. The scarabs ran past, below them.

"They almost got us!" said O'Connell. "Evelyn, I said . . ."

But Evelyn wasn't there. She lost O'Connell and Jonathan when they ran up the stairs. She walked into a dark room, below them. Where was she? She didn't know.

"O'Connell!" Evelyn shouted. "O'Connell!"

Then, she saw one of the Americans. He had his back to her, but it was Burns.

"Oh hello!" said Evelyn.

Burns turned around and she screamed. Burns had no eyes. He fell on the ground. Evelyn turned away, but she came face-to-face with . . .

Imhotep.

Imhotep, with Burns's blue eyes.

Imhotep couldn't see very well because Burns had to wear glasses. He looked at Evelyn.

"Anck-su-namun?" he said.

"Help me," Evelyn said to Burns.

But Burns couldn't see, and he could do nothing.

"*Kadeesh pharos Anck-su-namun,*" said Imhotep.

Evelyn was very afraid. "*I'm going to die,*" she thought. "*Please, somebody help me!*"

Suddenly, O'Connell ran in with a gun in his hand.

"Oh, there you are!" he said to Evelyn. "Where . . . ?"

"I'm going to die."

He saw Imhotep. He shot Imhotep and pulled Evelyn to him. Then, he took Evelyn's hand in his hand, and they ran.

Ardeth Bay and ten Med-Jai soldiers stopped them.

"I told you before: leave this place or die," said Ardeth Bay.

"It's OK," said O'Connell. "I shot the mummy. No problem!"

"A gun can't kill Imhotep!" said Ardeth Bay. He was very angry. "Now get out of here! All of you!"

Med-Jai soldiers found the Americans and Jonathan, and they all went back above ground. Only one person wasn't there. Beni was below the ground. He was with Imhotep.

"I can use you," Imhotep told Beni, in Egyptian. "And I will give you gold."

"Y— Yes," said Beni.

"I want the box with Anck-su-namun's heart," Imhotep told him.

◆

Above ground, Med-Jai soldiers helped Burns walk to a horse.

"What did you do to him?" shouted Henderson, the third American. "Look at his eyes."

"We helped him," said Ardeth Bay. "Now leave here before Imhotep kills everybody."

They all got on their horses. They wanted to get away from Imhotep.

"I got him," said O'Connell. "I told you, I shot this Imhotep."

But nobody listened to him. Nobody could kill Imhotep with a gun.

◆

Back in Cairo, Evelyn and O'Connell took Burns to his hotel room. Then, they went to O'Connell's room. They sat and shouted angrily.

"Let's go, Evelyn! We're out of here!" shouted O'Connell.

"No we are *not*!" shouted Evelyn. "We started this. Now we'll kill Imhotep and finish it."

"WE!" shouted O'Connell. "WE? *You* read from the *Book of the Dead*. And nobody can kill this Imhotep. Not with a gun. I tried."

"Then, we'll kill him some other way," said Evelyn.

A white cat came into the room and jumped on the bed.

O'Connell started to say something, but then, they heard a scream from Burns's room.

Imhotep was in Burns's room with Beni. He wanted Burns's heart. He had to have it so he could come back to life. And he took it. Burns gave one scream. Then, he was dead on the floor.

"Oh no!" cried Evelyn, when she and O'Connell ran into Burns's room.

O'Connell took out his gun. He and Evelyn watched Imhotep. He had new life, with Burns's heart inside him.

"We have a problem," said O'Connell.

Imhotep wanted Evelyn. He moved to her. O'Connell shot him again and again, but nothing happened. Imhotep threw O'Connell across the room. He fell on the floor in front of Jonathan, Henderson, and Daniels, when they ran in.

Imhotep spoke to Evelyn. "You gave me my life," he said. "I thank you."

He moved his face close to her and almost kissed her. But suddenly, the white cat ran into the room. Imhotep saw it and he was afraid. He stopped kissing Evelyn and ran out of the room.

"What happened?" asked O'Connell.

"The priests in Seti's time had white cats," said Evelyn. "The cats sat at the doors of the afterlife."

"That's good," said O'Connell. "But we have big problems."

Henderson looked at Burns, on the floor.

"Am I next?" he said. "I was in the room when we found that book."

"And me," said Daniels.

Imhotep moved his face close to her and almost kissed her.

"I have an idea," said Evelyn. "*The Book of the Dead* gave Imhotep life. We want him dead, so . . ."

"So the other book . . ." said Jonathan.

"Yes, the *Book of Amun Ra* can send him back to the underworld," said Evelyn. "The *Book Of Amun Ra* is at Hamunaptra but *where* in Hamunaptra? The museum! Let's go to the museum. We can find the answer there."

"I'll wait here," said Henderson.

"Me too," said Daniels.

Henderson went back to his hotel room. Daniels went back to his room, too. He looked at the gold box and smiled.

◆

Outside, the scarabs were everywhere. And more and more people came back to half-life. They were mummies and they followed

Imhotep. The streets were full of the undead. They walked slowly and they repeated Imhotep's name again and again.

Jonathan, Evelyn, and O'Connell walked to Jonathan's car and drove slowly to the museum. The undead looked into the car, but Jonathan didn't stop.

At the museum, they found the curator. Ardeth Bay was with him!

"This is the end of the world," said Ardeth Bay. "We cannot stop the undead and we cannot stop Imhotep."

Evelyn looked at book after book. She read for hours. And then . . .

"This is it! The *Book of Amun Ra* is in the statue of the god Horus."

"Let's go," shouted O'Connell.

◆

The scarabs were everywhere.

O'Connell, Evelyn, Jonathan, the curator, and Ardeth Bay drove back to the hotel and went to Henderson's room. He was dead. But Daniels was OK and he ran with them back to the car. He had his gold box with him.

Back in the car, Jonathan drove slowly. The undead were everywhere in the streets. There were hundreds of them. They shouted, "Imhotep, Imhotep." Then, they looked into the car and saw the box.

Jonathan drove fast, but the undead stopped the car. Daniels shot at them again and again. But more of the undead walked to the car. "Imhotep, Imhotep." They looked at Daniels with dead eyes. Then, they took him out of the car and killed him.

It was quiet in the car for a minute. Then, the undead came for O'Connell, Jonathan, Evelyn, the curator, and Ardeth Bay.

"*This is not good*," Evelyn thought.

Then, she saw him.

Imhotep.

But the new Imhotep was a young man with new life.

"He's beautiful," Evelyn said.

O'Connell didn't like that.

The undead took the gold box and gave it to Imhotep. Beni was with him. Evelyn, O'Connell, and the other men got out of the car.

"Wait!" said Imhotep to the undead.

The undead waited. Imhotep walked to Evelyn.

"Do you have any ideas?" Evelyn asked O'Connell.

"I'm thinking, I'm thinking," he said.

Imhotep put out his hand to Evelyn.

"I am living because of you," he said. "Come with me."

"He has Anck-su-namun's heart," said Ardeth Bay. "Now he wants your heart, too, so he can bring her back from the undead."

Imhotep's hand closed around Evelyn's. Evelyn turned to O'Connell.

Evelyn, O'Connell, and the other men got out of the car.

"I give my heart to you," she said. "But please come for it before he takes it out."

O'Connell almost smiled at that. "Yes, ma'am," he said.

Imhotep took Evelyn away. Then, he turned and shouted to the undead, "Kill them all!"

"Run!" shouted Ardeth Bay.

The head of the Med-Jai called for his soldiers. He took his sword and fought with the undead. The curator fought, too, but the undead killed him.

O'Connell and Jonathan ran.

"We can't leave Ardeth Bay!" shouted Jonathan.

"Yes, we can," said O'Connell. "We're going to Hamunaptra. We're going to find that statue and the book."

Chapter 5   The *Book of Amun Ra*

"How do we know this god?" asked O'Connell.

"Horus?" said Jonathan. "He has a big nose. Look for a big bird. That will be him."

"OK," said O'Connell. "Where do we start?"

He looked at the houses and the temple in Hamunaptra. He had no ideas.

◆

Below O'Connell and Jonathan, Beni had a gun in Evelyn's back. Imhotep was in front of them.

"Walk," said Beni.

"You'll die in the end," said Evelyn.

"I will?" said Beni.

"Oh, yes," said Evelyn, but she walked.

They came to the *Sah-Netjer.*

At the same time, Ardeth Bay and the Med-Jai were on their way across the desert.

◆

When Jonathan and O'Connell went down under the ground near the statue of Anubis, Imhotep heard them. He took some water from the gold box with Anck-su-numan's heart in it and threw it at a wall. His mummified priests, from 3,000 years before, walked in.

"Find them," said Imhotep.

Jonathan and O'Connell found the statue of Horus. Then, the mummified priests found them. Ardeth Bay and his soldiers came in and fought with the mummified priests.

"Does anybody have a white cat?" asked Jonathan.

"Find the book!" shouted Ardeth Bay.

◆

Back in the *Sah-Netjer*, Evelyn was in a coffin. The coffin was open, but she couldn't move her arms or her legs. In the next coffin was the mummy of Anck-su-namun. Imhotep sang. He had the *Book of the Dead* in one hand and he put the other hand on Anck-su-namun's dead face.

" *This is a love story*," thought Evelyn. " *He loved her for 3,000 years. And now I'm going to die for his love.*"

◆

Ardeth Bay and his soldiers fought hard, but there were more and more mummies. When they shot a mummy in the arm, the arm came off. Then, *it* fought, too. Jonathan and O'Connell didn't stop digging.

And then . . . then, they found a gold box, and in the gold box there was the *Book of Amun Ra*. It was beautiful, but they couldn't look at it now.

"Take the book and help the girl," Ardeth Bay shouted.

◆

Imhotep read from the *Book of the Dead*.

"When you die," he told Evelyn, "Anck-su-namun will live. And I will never die."

Anck-su-namun's eyes opened. Imhotep opened the coffin and took a knife. He stood with it over Evelyn's heart. This was the end.

Suddenly, O'Connell and Jonathan ran into the room. Imhotep turned to them.

" I found it, Evy ! " Jonathan shouted. He showed her the *Book of Amun Ra.* " I found it ! "

"Stop talking ! " Evelyn shouted at her brother. " Get me out of here ! "

Imhotep put the knife down . . . and walked to Jonathan.

" Open the book, Jonathan," Evelyn shouted. " That's the only way."

31

Jonathan tried, but he couldn't open it.

"Is there a key?" he asked.

Imhotep smiled. He had the key. He moved nearer to Jonathan. O'Connell took a sword from a statue's hand and started to cut into Evelyn's coffin.

"*Imhotep's going to kill Jonathan*," thought Evelyn. She thought quickly. "Jonathan, are there any words on the front of the book?"

Jonathan ran away from Imhotep and looked at the book at the same time.

"Words?" he said. "Yes."

O'Connell started to break the coffin. Imhotep turned and called the mummified priests back into the *Sah-Netjer*.

Jonathan tried to read the Egyptian writing on the front of the *Book of Amun Ra*. Why didn't he listen carefully in Egyptian classes at school?

O'Connell pulled Evelyn from the coffin. Jonathan read the words.

"*Rasheen . . . ooloo . . . Kashka!*" he said.

The big doors to the room opened. Ten mummified soldiers walked into the room. A new kind of mummy—worse than the other soldiers.

"Tell the soldiers that you're the boss," said Evelyn.

"Who? ME?" said Jonathan.

"Finish the words on the front of the book, you stupid boy."

"Oh yes!" said Jonathan. "The book, the book."

◆

Above Jonathan, in a room full of gold, Beni was a happy man. Here was the gold of the Pharaohs. He carried a lot of gold up to his big, white horse and put it in some bags on the horse. Then, he went down again for more gold.

◆

Below, in the *Sah-Netjer*, Imhotep walked to Jonathan and looked down at him. Jonathan looked at the book.

"I can't read this," he screamed to Evelyn. "This Egyptian letter... There are two lines at the top. One line at the bottom. There's a little..."

"It's an *ankh*," said Evelyn.

"Ah."

Soldier mummies fought with O'Connell. He was on the ground. Their swords were above him.

"*Hootash im Ahmenophus*," shouted Jonathan.

The soldier mummies stopped. Imhotep looked back at them. The soldier mummies looked at Jonathan.

"Why are you looking at me?" Jonathan asked them.

"You're their boss now," shouted Evelyn. "Tell them."

"Tell them what?" said Jonathan.

Anck-su-namun started to get up from her coffin. She wanted her life. She hit Evelyn again and again. Evelyn screamed.

"Jonathan!" screamed Evelyn. "Tell the soldiers... Stop her!"

"Oh. Yes. Right," said Jonathan. And then, "*Fa-kooshka Anck-su-namun*."

Anck-su-namun took her knife and put it above Evelyn's heart. But the soldier mummies jumped across the room and killed her. Imhotep screamed when he saw the love of his life die again. He jumped on Jonathan and took the *Book of Amun Ra* from his hands.

"Now, you die," he said.

O'Connell ran across the room and cut Imhotep's arm off with the statue's sword. Imhotep smiled. Nobody could kill him. He took Jonathan in his other hand.

"OK, so he can fight with his left hand," said O'Connell.

But the *Book of Amun Ra* was now on the floor and the key was on the floor, too. Evelyn got out of the coffin and ran to the key. She opened the book.

Soldier mummies fought with O'Connell.

O'Connell pulled Imhotep away from Jonathan. Imhotep turned and threw O'Connell across the room.

Evelyn looked into the *Book of Amun Ra*.

"Can you fight with Imhotep for three or four minutes? Please!" she shouted to O'Connell.

Imhotep threw O'Connell across the room again with his one arm.

"No problem," O'Connell answered.

Imhotep took O'Connell's sword.

"You are going to die!" he said.

Evelyn read from the gold book.

"*Kadeesh mal!*" she shouted. "*Kadeesh mal! Pareed oos! PAREED OOS!*"

Imhotep turned. He was very afraid. How did she know these words? They were the end for him.

The god Anubis came into the room. He walked through Imhotep and left again. Imhotep was now a man, only a man.

And a man can die. O'Connell took the sword and pushed it through Imhotep. And Imhotep, the man, died. But he said something before he died.

He said, "This is not the end."

◆

Above them, Beni found gold on the wall of a room. His eyes opened. He smiled. He took out his knife and pulled the gold off the wall. The room came down on top of him. He remembered Evelyn's words: "You'll die in the end."

"Yes," said Beni. And he died.

◆

"Run," shouted O'Connell. "The place is coming down!"

Jonathan, Evelyn, and O'Connell ran up, above ground, and Hamunaptra fell back into the desert behind them. Now there was nothing there.

"From all my people, I thank you."

They found three horses and got on them. Then, they started across the desert, away from Hamunaptra.

A hand fell on Jonathan's arm. Jonathan screamed.

"Oh, it's you!" he said. "Thank you very much."

"No! I thank *you*," said Ardeth Bay. He looked at O'Connell and Evelyn. "From all my people, I thank you. Imhotep is dead and now there are no undead or scarabs in the city of Cairo."

"Oh that's OK, my friend!" said Jonathan. "*Thanks are fine,*" he thought, "*but we didn't get any gold.*"

Ardeth Bay smiled and went off into the desert.

"My horse is walking slowly," said Jonathan. Then, he stopped and looked in the bags on the big, white horse. "Evelyn!" he shouted. "Gold!"

But Evelyn was busy. She put her arms around O'Connell and they kissed.

Maybe this wasn't the end. Maybe it was the beginning.

ACTIVITIES

Chapter 1

Before you read

1 Read the Introduction to the book. What do you know about Egypt in the time of the pharaohs? Do you like books and movies about this time?

2 Did you see the movie of *The Mummy*? What do you remember of the story?

3 Look at the Word List at the back of the book.
  a Find new words in your dictionary.
  b Which word goes with which other word? Why?
     brain   curator   heart   high priest   museum   soldier   sword   temple

While you read

4 What happens first? What happens next? Write the numbers 1–8.
  a Imhotep cuts out Anck-su-namun's heart.   5
  b The Pharaoh finds Imhotep with Anck-su-namun.   1
  c Imhotep reads from the *Book of the Dead*.   6
  d Imhotep kills the Pharaoh.   3
  e Scarabs start to eat Imhotep.   8
  f Anck-su-namun pushes a sword into her heart.   2
  g Imhotep takes his dead lover to Hamunaptra.   4
  h The Med-Jai break the box with the heart in it.   7

After you read

5 Answer these questions.
  a Why can't Anck-su-namun be Imhotep's lover?
  b Why does Imhotep send Anck-su-namun to the underworld?
  c What does the *Book of Amun Ra* do?
  d What does the *Book of the Dead* do?
  e Why do the Med-Jai have to watch Imhotep?

6 In the next chapter, the story moves into the future. Discuss these questions with another student.
  a Will the story move to today, or to an earlier time?
  b Will Imhotep live again? How can this happen?

c What new people will be in the story?

d Which countries will they come from?

Chapter 2

Before you read

7 Look at the pictures on pages 7 and 8 and discuss these questions.

   a Do you think that Rick O'Connell looks dangerous (page 7)? What is strange about his guns?

   b What is Beni's job (page 8)?

While you read

8 Write one word in each sentence.

   a In Hamunaptra, some soldiers are fighting for ....

   b O'Connell is from ....

   c Beni is from ....

   d Evelyn Carnahan works in the Cairo ....

   e She comes from ....

   f Her brother Jonathan is .... years old.

   g Ardeth Bay is the head of the ....

After you read

9 Answer these questions. Who:

   a took some gold from a temple?

   b falls on the floor with some old books?

   c brings a box to the museum?

   d puts a map on a candle?

   e found a box in Hamunaptra?

   f was on a mountain when O'Connell ran away?

10 After they leave the curator's office, Evelyn and Jonathan finish their conversation. Work with another student.

   Student A: You are Evelyn. You want to know more about the map and Rick O'Connell. Ask Jonathan about O'Connell. What does he think of him? Why did he take the map from him?

   Student B: You are Jonathan. Answer Evelyn's questions. Tell her about O'Connell and the map.

Chapter 3

Before you read

11 Discuss these questions.
   a Who will go to Hamunaptra?
   b What will they find there?

While you read

12 Who is speaking?
   a "Can I help you down from that horse?"   ....
   b "He's here for the gold."   ....
   c "Sometimes people find Hamunaptra,
       but they all die."   ....
   d "*We* want to look here."   ....
   e "This is *our* statue, friend."   ....
   f "Leave this place or die!"   ....
   g "What did that writing on the box say?"   ....
   h "People read books all the time."   ....

After you read

13 Talk to another student. Look at the people in the pictures on pages 14 and 19. What do you know about them?

14 Discuss these questions. What do you think?
   a Is Evelyn happy when she sees O'Connell outside the temple?
   b Is Beni a good friend of O'Connell's?
   c Why is Evelyn not happy with O'Connell and Jonathan when they go into the dark room?
   d Does Jonathan know much about Egypt in the time of Pharaoh Seti?
   e Does Jonathan know about guns?
   f Why does Evelyn say, "Let's be nice children and play nicely."

15 At the start of Chapter 3, Evelyn and Jonathan meet Rick O'Connell near the temple at Hamunaptra. Jonathan thinks that O'Connell is there for the gold. Evelyn doesn't know. Work with another student.
   Student A: You are Evelyn. You are starting to like this strange American man. Why is he here? What does he want to do? Ask him.

Student B: You are O'Connell. Answer Evelyn's questions. Why is she here? Ask her.

Chapter 4

Before you read

16 Which of these do you think that you will read about in this chapter?

a beach   a computer   a gold box   a gun   a horse
a mountain   a white cat   an airport   scarabs   television

17 In this chapter, three of the people below will die. Which people, do you think?

Ardeth Bay   Beni   Burns   Daniels   Evelyn   Henderson
Imhotep   Jonathan   O'Connell   the curator

While you read

18 Write the names of the people.

a Imhotep takes *his* eyes.   ....
b *He* has to get Anck-su-namun's heart
   for Imhotep.   ....
c Burns dies when *he* takes his heart.   ....
d The undead kill *him* and take the gold box.   ....
e Imhotep wants *her* heart.   ....
f *They* look for the statue of Horus and the
   Book of Amun Ra.   ....
                                                       ....

After you read

19 Answer these questions.

a Why can Imhotep not see very well?
b Why does Beni help Imhotep?
c Why is Imhotep afraid of the white cat?
d Why does Imhotep want Evelyn's heart?

20 Work with another student. Have this conversation.

Student A: You are Ardeth Bay, the head of the Med-Jai. The Med-Jai are thousands of years old, but now the world wants to know more about them. Student B works for a newspaper. Talk to him/her.

Student B: You work for a newspaper. Your readers want to know more about the Med-Jai. Also, ask Ardeth about Evelyn, O'Connell, and the other people from different countries. How does Ardeth feel about them?

Chapter 5

Before you read

21 Look at these sentences. What do you *want* to happen? What do you *think* will happen?

    a Imhotep will give Evelyn's heart to Anck-su-namun.

    b O'Connell and Jonathan will find the *Book of Amun Ra*.

    c O'Connell will kill Imhotep.

    d Evelyn and O'Connell will marry.

    e Evelyn and Beni will marry.

    f Imhotep will bring Anck-su-namun back and marry her.

    g Beni will die.

While you read

22 Are these sentences right (✓) or wrong (✗)?

    a Imhotep likes white cats. .....

    b Jonathan learned Egyptian at school. .....

    c O'Connell takes the key from Imhotep. .....

    d The god Anubis changes Imhotep. .....

    e Beni dies because he loves gold. .....

    f Jonathan's horse walks slowly because it is old. .....

After you read

23 Work with another student. Finish these sentences. How many possible answers can you think of?

    a Jonathan is happy at the end of the story because …

    b Evelyn and O'Connell are happy because …

    c Ardeth Bay is happy because …

    d Imhotep died because …

    e Anck-su-namun died because …

24 In this book, and in the movie, Imhotep's last words are, "This is not the end." Why are these words important to the story and to the makers of the movie?

Writing

25 You are Imhotep. You are half-dead and stay in the ground for thousands of years. You are thinking. How did this happen to you? Tell your story.

26 Look at the photo on page 8. Beni is fighting for France, but he is Hungarian. Many soldiers from other countries wore clothes like this and fought for France in the "Foreign Legion." What do you know about them? Find out and write about them.

27 Evelyn and O'Connell are very different. She works in a museum and he is a soldier. She wants to learn new things about Egypt and he wants to have a good time. Are they going to be happy? Write about this.

28 Ardeth Bay and the Med-Jai live outside today's world. Do you think that this is possible? Think about people in deserts and other quiet places. How are their lives changing? For how long can they have a different way of life? Write about this.

29 A year after the story ends, Evelyn writes a letter to Jonathan. Where is she? What is she doing? Who is she with? Write her letter.

30 Look at a photo in the book. What can you see? What is happening at this time in the story? What is going to happen? Write about it.

31 Find a photo in the book with two or more people in it. Write their conversation.

32 Which person do you like best in the story? Why do you like them? Write about this person.

WORD LIST *with example sentences*

brain (n) Where did you leave your books? Think! Use your *brain*!

candle (n) There were no lights in the bedrooms. People used *candles.*

coffin (n) We are going to buy a *coffin* because our father died yesterday.

curator (n) I don't know what these old things are. Let's ask the *curator.*

desert (n) After ten days in the *desert*, he had to find water.

dig (v) Why is the dog *digging* under the trees? Is it looking for something?

god (n) Eros was the Greek *god* of love.

gold (n/adj) People went to California in the 1840s because they wanted to find *gold.*

heart (n) His *heart* stopped and he died.

high priest (n) In the past, all Egyptians had to listen to the *high priests.*

key (n) This is the *key* to our front door.

kiss (v) *Kiss* your mother before you go out!

mummy (n) You can see the *mummy* of Ramses II in Cairo. It is very, very old.

museum (n) There are a lot of *museums* in London, but the British Museum is the most famous.

scarab (n) You can find *scarabs*' eggs under the ground, often in very dirty places.

scream (n/v) A car hit him. I heard the *scream.*

soldier (n) *Soldiers* from many countries are fighting in Afghanistan.

statue (n) There is a *statue* of Horatio Nelson in Trafalgar Square, in London.

sword (n) He pulled out a *sword* and cut off the other man's arm.

temple (n) We visited a lot of Hindu *temples* when we were in India.